VOWEL ADVENTURES

ALAN PLAYS BALL
AN ADVENTURE WITH THE VOWEL A

by Brandon Terrell
illustrated by Daniela Massironi

GRASSHOPPER

Tools for Parents & Teachers

Grasshopper Books enhance imagination and introduce the earliest readers to fiction with fun storylines and illustrations. The easy-to-read text supports early reading experiences with repetitive sentence patterns and sight words.

Before Reading

- Look at the cover illustration. What do readers see? What do they think the book will be about?

- Look at the picture glossary together. Sound out the words. Ask readers to identify the first letter of each vocabulary word.

Read the Book

- "Walk" through the book, reading to or along with the reader. Point to the illustrations as you read.

After Reading

- Review the picture glossary again. Ask readers to locate the words in the text.

- Ask the reader: What does a short 'a' sound like? What does a long 'a' sound like? Which words did you see in the book with these sounds? What other words do you know that have these sounds?

Grasshopper Books are published by Jump!
5357 Penn Avenue South
Minneapolis, MN 55419
www.jumplibrary.com

Library of Congress Cataloging-in-Publication Data

Names: Terrell, Brandon, 1978-2021 author.
Massironi, Daniela, illustrator.
Title: Alan plays ball: an adventure with the vowel a by Brandon Terrell; illustrated by Daniela Massironi.
Description: Minneapolis, MN: Jump!, Inc., [2022]
Series: Vowel adventures
Includes reading tips and supplementary back matter.
Audience: Ages 5-7.
Identifiers: LCCN 2020058567 (print)
LCCN 2020058568 (ebook)
ISBN 9781636902371 (hardcover)
ISBN 9781636902388 (paperback)
ISBN 9781636902395 (ebook)
Subjects: LCSH: Readers (Primary)
Classification: LCC PE1119.2 .T47 2022 (print)
LCC PE1119.2 (ebook) | DDC 428.6/2—dc23
LC record available at https://lccn.loc.gov/2020058567
LC ebook record available at https://lccn.loc.gov/2020058568

Editor: Eliza Leahy
Direction and Layout: Anna Peterson
Illustrator: Daniela Massironi

Printed in the United States of America at Corporate Graphics in North Mankato, Minnesota.

Brandon M. Terrell (B.1978-D.2021) was a talented storyteller, authoring more than 100 books for children. He was a passionate reader, Star Wars enthusiast, amazing father, and devoted husband. This book is dedicated in his memory. Happy reading!

Table of Contents

Play Ball!

Alan is a fan of playing ball.

"I can play *any* sport!" Alan boasts.

Alan plays baseball.

He takes a bat. He smacks the ball.

CRACK!

"What a hit!" Alan says.

Alan plays in a
basketball game.

"Watch me make a basket!"
Alan brags.

Air ball!

"Aw, man!" Alan says sadly.

Alan also plays tennis.

He grabs a racket.
He swats at the ball.

THWAP!

It sails past Anna!
It lands far away.

"That was a bit extra,"
Alan says.

Alan laces up skates.

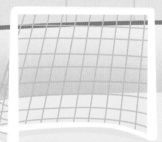

Alan flails on the ice.

"Whoa!" He falls backward.

Alan takes a chance at soccer.

A player passes the ball.

TAP!

The ball accidentally
hits Alan's head.

The ball lands in the net.

That's the game!

Fans clap.

Alan's team celebrates.

"I really *can* play any sport!" Alan says.

Let's Review Vowel A!

Point to the words with the short 'a' sound you saw in the book.
Point to the words with the long 'a' sound.

play　　　**crack**　　　**clap**　　　**skates**　　　**game**　　　**passes**

Picture Glossary

accidentally
Not on purpose,
or without
meaning to.

boasts
Brags about
something
in order to
impress people.

celebrates
Does something
special to mark
a happy occasion.

flails
Moves or
swings one's
arms or legs.